Arduino 2020 Guide

With Easy Twelve Projects to Get Started

Introduction

Getting Started With Arduino
Start by Programming the Arduino Uno Board
Your First Example LED Blink (Hello Embedded World)

Arduino Analog Input with Temperature Sensor
Components
Circuit
Software

Generate Tones With Arduino
Components and Circuit
Simulation and Code
Build Real Circuit

Arduino Mario Theme with Arduino
Hardware Components
Connections and Circuit
Code and Software
Test Your Circuit and Play Mario Theme

Why Do We Need To Turn a Smartphone Into a Virtual Arduino Board?
Option 1: Android App That Programs Arduino Board Without Having a PC
Option 2: Android App That Controls Arduino Board
Option 3: 1sheeld - Turn Your Smartphone Into Multiple Shields
What I Really Want: Android Replacing Arduino Hardware

Cricket Sounds With Arduino
Components
Program the Code
Connect the Circuit and Run

Smartphone Bluetooth Controlled PWM Light
 Components
 Circuit
 Upload Arduino Code
 Run the App and Control Your Arduino

Arduino Bluetooth RGB Mood Light
 Hardware Components
 Circuit Connection
 RemoteXY Editor
 Software Generation
 Final Interface
 Operational Test

Connect Arduino to USB Keyboard
 The Story
 The USB Female Port
 Circuit Connection
 Software
 Attachments
 Test the Project

Simple Drive a 220V Relay With Arduino
 Supplies:
 Drive a Relay With a Transistor - Transistor As a Switch
 Circuit
 Get the Parts
 Prepare and Start Assembling
 Connect to Arduino, Upload Software and Run the Test

Clone Arduino UNO Into ATtiny85 Microcontroller
 Install ATiny on Arduino IDE
 Programming Circuit - Connect ATtiny to Arduino UNO

Prepare Arduino UNO to Be an ISP Programmer

Burn the Bootloader

Upload the Blink Sketch - or Just Any Other Sketch

Test Your New ATtiny Arduino

Connect Arduino with GSM Shield SIM900

Supplies

Choosing Power Supply Source

Power ON the Module and Automatic Powering

AT Commands

Receiving a Call

Making a Call

Supply Power to Arduino

Introduction

Arduino has become a popular platform for both professionals and enthusiasts.

That's because it's an open source, simple and collaborative effort based project. You can make virtually anything with Arduino.

You can start learning it from scratch using minimal tools. And then you can find code for whatever project and peripherals your project needs.

With minimum code writing and editing you can get your complete application ready in minutes.

This book is a quick reference for getting you started with Arduino using rapid deployment methods of trying different peripherals and tricks with Arduino.

This is not a theoretical book but it's a compilation of practical yet simple Arduino projects for a quick jump start.

You are encouraged to try as many projects as you like to get the most out of this book.

Thank you for starting this journey with us and hope you enjoy it.

Getting Started With Arduino

This is the first project so I decided to introduce it as part of my tutorials.

In each project we'll deal with one Arduino/Arduino Compatible board with simple steps that can get you started even if you are a complete beginner.

If you want to learn Arduino then you need to get your hands busy. So Let's get started.

Start by Programming the Arduino Uno Board

Programming

What you need:

Arduino Uno Board

USB Cable

Arduino IDE (download and setup on your computer)

Your First Example LED Blink (Hello Embedded World)

I know this is so primitive but if you are a beginner this is really rewarding.

If you manage to blink an LED in one system then you can do anything else.

Open Arduino IDE. From the menu choose ….

Tools -- Board -- Arduino Uno

Then you can see the code that blinks the built in LED in your Arduino board.

Choose **Menu**

File – Upload

File – Examples – Basics – Blink.

Now you can see the LED in Arduino board blinking at a constant rate.

Congratulations.

You have completed the very first Arduino lesson.

Now you are ready to test more projects.

Arduino Analog Input with Temperature Sensor

Now you have an Arduino board, what can you do with it ?

Very simple temperature sensor project.

I got an analog temperature sensor from Texas Instruments **TMP01FPZ**. I bought an Arduino UNO compatible board. I wanted to make a simple circuit to use both.

Here it is.

Components

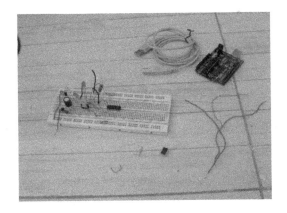

Arduino UNO and its cable

TMP01FPZ Temperature Sensor

Bread Board

Some small wires or Alligator clips

Circuit

 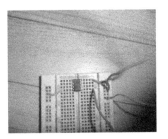

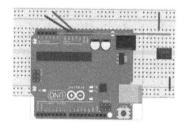 

The circuit is very simple.

Just connect the Vcc and GND pins of the Temperature Sensor TMP01FPZ to the +5 v and GND pins of the Arduino UNO board to get it powered by 5 volts.

Then connect the analog out pin of the sensor to pin A0 of the Arduino UNO.

Software

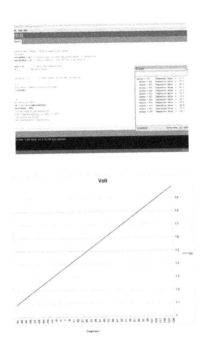

Configure the Analog input pin A0.

Read the analog input value to the variable **sensorValue**

Convert the analog input raw count into useful temperature degrees Celsius according to the datasheet of the sensor.

The chart represents the sensor response (output voltage) to temperature as described in the datasheet.

Send the output degrees to the serial output on the USB port.

Read the output on the serial monitor.

You can download Arduino code from here.

Generate Tones With Arduino

In this project I made a circuit that generates tone with Arduino. I really like simple and fast to build projects. Here is a simple project of this kind.

https://www.arduino.cc/en/Tutorial/ToneMelody?from=Tutorial.Tone

In this project, I've tried to generate tones with Arduino board.

Using Arduino Uno and an 8 ohm speaker, you can easily generate tones and sounds.

This Arduino sketch uses Tone function to generate sounds.

Components and Circuit

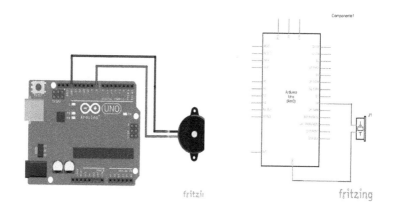

Components:

Arduino Uno or any other Arduino board will do.

8 Ohm Speaker

Prototyping Breadboard

Connection circuit:

The circuit is very simple.

Connect the speaker to Arduino board on PIN 8
and GND.

Simulation and Code

Simulation is a great tool to test your design before actually building anything. You can also use simulation when you don't have the hardware and you need to get started.

In this simple circuit, simulation is only used for clarifying the concept and showing how it works.

There are many Arduino simulation software. In this project, I used Autodesk online platform Tinkercad.

You can see the circuit and start simulation. You can edit it and change the code to your needs.

https://www.tinkercad.com/things/fWelGEvtEDT-start-simulating

You can build any circuit you like and you can also browse all projects to find what you are looking for. You can download the code tones.ino from <u>here</u> and the pitches.h from <u>here</u>.

Build Real Circuit

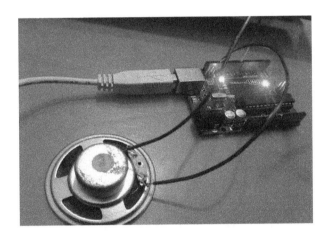

Now you can build the real circuit and upload Arduino sketch to the board.

Arduino Mario Theme with Arduino

Who doesn't love that Mario Theme? We all love that epic game and like to see over and over.

Today we can see this fast built circuit that uses an Arduino to play Mario Theme.

You can typically build this circuit in only 5 minutes.

My tribe knows me and realizes that I'm short on time. That's why I like fast built projects.

In this project, you can learn to play long tones using only Arduino Uno and a speaker.

Let's get started.

Hardware Components

What you need:

Arduino Uno Board

USB Cable

8 Ohm Speaker

Arduino IDE (download and setup on your computer)

Connections and Circuit

 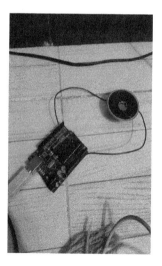

The circuit is very simple.

This circuit uses PWM signals from PIN 3 to generate tones.

Then all you have to do is to connect the speaker to PIN 3 and GND on your Arduino Board.

Code and Software

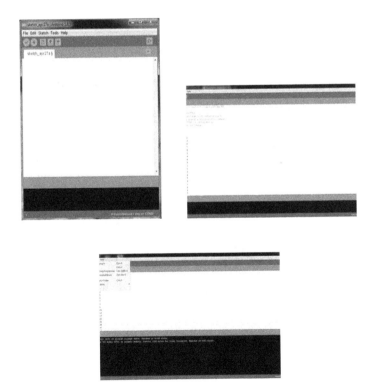

Now open Arduino IDE and paste this code inside it.

Download the code from here.

Compile the code.

Upload the sketch into your Arduino board.

Play your favorite Mario Theme and enjoy.

Test Your Circuit and Play Mario Theme

Now you can play your favorite Mario Theme on Arduino.

Why Do We Need To Turn a Smartphone Into a Virtual Arduino Board?

Arduino emulator on Android

Run Arduino code on Android smartphone

Connect Android smartphone to Arduino IDE

In this project I'm searching for a solution to a problem I faced today.

I thought about it and tried to search it all over the internet and still couldn't find it yet.

My idea is that I want to find an Arduino Emulator that runs on an Android Smartphone.

I've searched the internet but still could find one.

To make it clear.

Emulator is different that a Simulator.

Simulator is a software that can run Arduino code and make it visual to you apparently. But *Emulator* is running the code with the ability to make outside world FEEL as if a real Arduino is running the code.

Think of it.

All of the following options are the things already there and I don't mean any of them.

Option 1: Android App That Programs Arduino Board Without Having a PC

Parts needed:

- Smartphone with Arduino IDE App
- USB OTG support Real Arduino Board

In this case, you need to have an

Android smartphone, tablet or phablet that has USB OTG feature and runs Arduino IDE so you can write code on it and then download it on a real Arduino board.

Good idea, but that's not what I need.

Option 2: Android App That Controls Arduino Board

Parts needed:

- PC running Arduino IDE to program the Arduino Board

- Smartphone with control interface App

- Real Arduino Board

- Bluetooth Module for Arduino

In this case, you need to have a real Arduino board that connects to Android device and that Android device runs an app has interface for controlling Arduino PINs and LEDs.

For example, **Blynk** is a great platform to create Androids Apps that can control Arduino via Bluetooth and WiFi.

You can also find many applications on Google Play.

Another brilliant idea, but that's not what I want either.

Option 3: 1sheeld - Turn Your Smartphone Into Multiple Shields

Parts needed:

- PC running Arduino IDE

- Smartphone with 1Sheeld App

- Real Arduino Board

- 1Sheeld Board

This project made by Egyptian group of engineers called 1sheeld.

This project makes something close to what I want but instead of using the USB cable to connect smartphone to PC they use a special built Arduino shield that connects Arduino to Android via Bluetooth.

Here you still need the real Arduino board. Also, the Arduino code is run on a real Arduino board but you only used Android as an extension shield for Arduino.

Here comes the famous slogan of 1sheeld "replace all you Arduino shields with only 1sheeld".

This is a great solution indeed, but that's not what I am looking for.

What I Really Want: Android Replacing Arduino Hardware

Parts needed:

PC running Arduino IDE Smartphone with Emulator App

USB cable (Mini USB for smartphone) A PC running Arduino IDE

and Android device running emulator app and they are both connected with a USB cable.

When the app on Android starts and connects to PC, the PC detects as if an Arduino board is connected to COM 4 for example. I want to write, verify and compile Arduino sketches on the PC and then upload the code to the Android device. Then the Android device can run the code and performs all android functions.

For example, the Android device has some LEDs that can be turned on and off when I write Arduino code for them. Android has an LCD display that can write text on it.

Android accelerometer and gyroscope can send serial data to the PC on the serial monitor. In short, I want to use mobile phones and standard PC to write code and run it without having to carry an Arduino board.

If you see that application, please leave a comment or send me a message.

Cricket Sounds With Arduino

The cricket is a little bug that makes noise at night.

Some people find them annoying. But some others -and I'm one of them- find them soothing and a symbol of nature and piece.

I admit that this repeatable sound of cricket can be annoying. It might get you sleep deprivation specially if it keeps making this noise in a place near where you sleep.

But the other type of people who find its sound soothing may be grateful to hear it at bedtime and feel relaxed from it.

There are even some iPhone and Android apps that do nothing but playing those sounds to keep you relaxed.

Today I thought of generating these sound using Arduino for fun.

This can be a good way of relaxation and you don't need to go look for that cricket if you want it to stop. In this case you can simply turn it off.

After all you are the one who programmed it.

I found a good project from a clever guy who made the most annoying cricket sound ever.

He wanted to make it a prank for his friend that he made the sound generation at random intervals.

He also made a consistent version of sound that sounded just like the normal cricket does.

In this version you can control the volume using PWM Pulse Width Modulation.

I liked the consistent sound version.

So here is how I made it.

Components

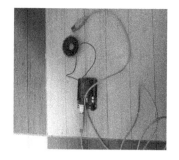

What you'll need:

Arduino board

8 ohm speaker.

Wires to connect the speaker to Arduino board.

USB Arduino Cable

Program the Code

Program the software using Arduino IDE

Full software are available from the original page:

https://github.com/connornishijima/arduino-volume1/tree/master/examples/volume_crickeduino_prank

Connect the Circuit and Run

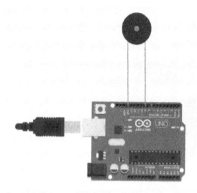

You can change the sound of the cricket as you like. The volume, times and randomness.

Smartphone Bluetooth Controlled PWM Light

In this project I'm going to show you how I made this simple Bluetooth Smartphone controlled PWM LED light for my kids. This is a simple but beautiful Arduino project to make.

I've used this awesome application ArduDroid from Mr. Hazim Bitar.

I really want to express my thanks to Mr. Hazim for this great app he has made available for us to control Arduino using Smartphone without writing a single line of code.

Components

Here are the components I used in my simple circuit.

Arduino UNO

HC-06 Bluetooth Module

LED

Arduino Cable

Some Jumper Wires

Circuit

 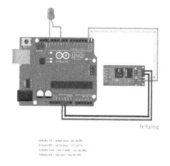

fritzing

Arduino TX - green wire - HC-06 RX
Arduino RX - red wire - HC-06 TX
Arduino GND - black wire - HC-06 GND
Arduino 5V - red wire - HC-06 +5V

The circuit is so simple. I connected the LED to Arduino PIN number 10. You can connect it to that PIN or to any other PIN that can generate Analog PWM signal.

Note: PWM PINS are marked with the ~ sign.

Then I connected the Bluetooth module to the Arduino UNO as follows

HC-06 Bluetooth module Arduino UNO

GND <-------> GND

VCC <-------> VCC

RX <-------> TX

TX <-------> RX

Note that you should not connect the Bluetooth Module to Arduino Board when Arduino is connected to the PC. This is because Arduino is connected to the PC on the same serial port on which Bluetooth Module is connected by default. And that can cause some weirdness in Arduino response during code uploading.

We can overcome this problem in future projects by changing the PINS on which Bluetooth is connected to Arduino UNO using Arduino function called SoftSerial().

But here we'll only connect Bluetooth Module after we upload the code and then connect the PC as a USB power source.

Upload Arduino Code

I just copied the code and then pasted it into Arduino IDE.

You can find the code at the application's website

http://www.techbitar.com/uploads/2/0/3/1/2031 6977/ardudroid.ino

Or download it from here.

Run the App and Control Your Arduino

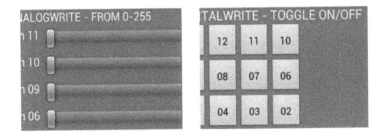

You can find that useful app from techbitar.com

http://www.techbitar.com/ardudroid-simple-bluetooth-control-for-arduino-and-android.html or from Google Play

https://play.google.com/store/apps/details?id=c om.techbitar.android.Andruino

Then you need to connect your Smartphone with the Bluetooth Module. You can do so by pressing the Connect to Bluetooth Button on the App.

Then choose your Bluetooth Module from the Bluetooth devices.

Once you have connected Bluetooth Module with the Smartphone you note that Bluetooth Module has its LED steady instead of flashing while not connected.

Now you can control LEDs from your Smartphone as follows:

The PIN 13 Red LED on the Arduino Board can be controlled ON/OFF using the PIN 13 Button on the App.

The LED you connected to PIN 10 can be controlled ON/OFF using the PIN 10 Button on the App.

The LED you connected to PIN 10 can be controlled Dimming using the PIN 10 Slider on the App.

Arduino Bluetooth RGB Mood Light

In this project I'll show you how to build a simple and complex Arduino Bluetooth projects you can control with your smartphone.

This is made simple with this smart application RemoteXY.

You can make your mood light, RC car, Quadcopter, Home Automation or any other project using this basic information to connect Arduino to your smartphone via Bluetooth connection.

All those projects can be made simple thanks to this genius application.

Here is a detailed step by step guide and code.

Hardware Components

Hardware required:

Arduino UNO Board

HC-06 Bluetooth Module

Red, Green and Blue LEDs

I connected the negative (shorter) leg of the three LEDs together for easy use.

Jumper wires

Circuit Connection

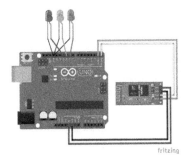

The connection is very simple.

You connect the Arduino Board to the Bluetooth Module via the hardware serial port(Pin #0 and Pin #1).

Arduino UNO <------> HC-06 Module

Vcc Vcc

GND GND

Tx Rx

Rx Tx

Connect LEDs as follows

Arduino UNO <------> LEDs

GND Common Short Legs

Pin # 9 Red LED +ve terminal (Longer Leg)

Pin # 10 Green LED +ve terminal (Longer Leg)

Pin # 11 Blue LED +ve terminal (Longer Leg)

RemoteXY Editor

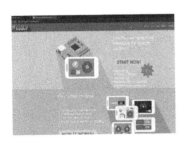

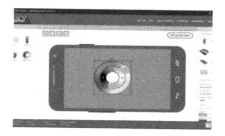

Configuration

Editor

Open Remote XY Editor at RemoteXY.com
and place controls. RGB control and Toggle
switch. Here is where you can design the
Smartphone interface.

Connection

Bluetooth

Device

Arduino UNO

Module

HC-06 Module

IDE

Arduino IDE

Module Interface

Select Hardware Serial

Speed(Baud Rate) 9600

View

You can configure controls appearance here.

Software Generation

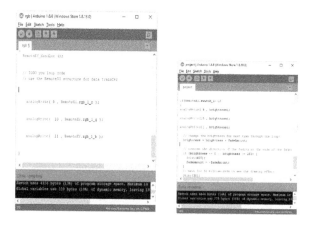

You need to download the generated code from the editor. You also need to include the Remote XY library from the same page.

Then you need to edit the code in Arduino IDE.

That's because the generated code only configures the controls. Then you need to code the actions between Arduino and those controls.

Final Interface

Download Remote XY App from Google Play or Apple Store.

Open it and connect to your device.

You can see the interface loads on your smartphone.

This is how the interface looks on the Smartphone.

Note:

You don't need to be connected to the internet for using this interface between the phone and Bluetooth Module.

Operational Test

Run the application and power up the device.

Try the different modes of operation.

In the RGB mode, you can control the output color using the RGB circular control.

In the MOOD mode, the light fades in and fades out automatically.

In this project, I made a quick light diffuser using a piece of white paper.

Get the code from <u>here</u> and RemoteXY library from <u>here</u>.

Connect Arduino to USB Keyboard

The actual sit and write is the essence of being a writer. Just as in any other discipline, if you do not invest time, mind and effort in doing it, you are treating it to be just a hobby.

The mind you give to the process of writing comes back to you in the form of the Flow. The process of effortlessly create something valuable with ease and timelessness. It's well known that whatever habit that you devote yourself to is what you can be finally rewarded for.

That's why I've wanted to make this project to concentrate on the process of writing itself.

The Story

Today I'm showing you how I've made this new project. Of course, it's about Arduino and it's about writing.

For some reason I wanted to connect Arduino to my keyboard.

Because I love writing on the keyboard.

It's that real physical feeling of switches on my fingertips that makes me feel creative and alive.

But there's only a small problem. My favorite keyboard is happened to a USB keyboard.

Yes that's the new modern technology is about and it's something I should be happy with.

But the only problem I was having when I wanted to connect my keyboard to Arduino (as a host to my keyboard) I found that the standard use of Arduino with a keyboard is the PS2 connection.

Actually there is a good well written Arduino library for this purpose.

So how could I connect my USB keyboard to Arduino? I only remembered back then when I was looking for a keyboard for my notebook (which had no PS2 ports in it) is that I wanted to figure out some way to use a PS2 keyboard with a USB port but I couldn't find this.

And that's why I bought the USB keyboard for the first place.

But this search has helped me a lot these days when I wanted to connect my USB keyboard to Arduino.

I then remembered that although I couldn't use a normal PS2 keyboard with a USB port in a notebook because of the different protocols, but the opposite is doable.

I remembered that I've found a project that described building a USB to PS2 converter.

The writer mentioned that he has tried it and it worked.

This means that you can use a modern USB keyboard with your old PCs and laptops using only this converter.

It's just a physical converter for the connection between the keyboard and the host port(not a voltage or protocol converter). That's because the USB keyboard can be powered from the old PS2 port, take the CLOCK signal from it and then send DATA signal to it.

And the writer has tried to make this setup and it worked. Now it was my turn. When I looked for some information to connect a USB to an Arduino board I found that in order to do this I need either an Arduino USB shield or an Arduino board with Microcontroller that have the native USB host physical feature. Neither option were available to me.

So I've decided to try the physical USB to PS2 converter - the writer has tried with his PC - between my USB keyboard and Arduino. You know what? This one also worked.

Using the PS2 Arduino library we can connect the USB keyboard directly to Arduino boards such as Arduino UNO or Arduino Mini.

The USB Female Port

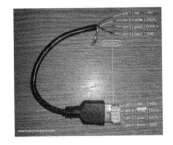
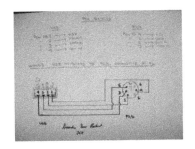

I had that female USB connector but I had to first test its pin-out with a voltmeter.

Then I made a cross connection between the USB connector and the PS2 keyboard of the library.

USB Keyboard PS2 Port

+5 v Vcc +5 v Vcc

Data- Data

Data+ Clock

GND GND

Circuit Connection

Components

Arduino UNO

Female USB port

Connection

USBPort Arduino

+5 v Vcc +5 v Vcc

Data- PIN 2

Data+ PIN 3

GND GND

Software

Software

Download and save the latest Arduino PS2 library from here.

Open Arduino IDE.

On the sketch menu, select library. Add Zip file.

Point to the Arduino PS2 library Zip file location and then press Enter.

On the File menu select examples.

From PS2keyboard sub-menu select International.

You find the international.ino sketch loaded into the Arduino IDE.

https://github.com/PaulStoffregen/PS2Keyboard

Edit these two lines of code

#include

const int DataPin = 8 ;

const int IRQpin = 5 ;

In this case, I used

DataPin to be Arduino Pin 2

and

IRQpin to be Arduino Pin 3

You can get the code from here. And PS/2
Keyboard library from here.

Test the Project

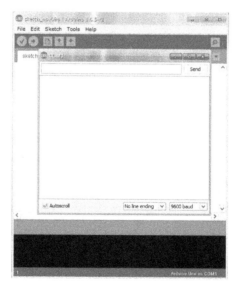

Open the Serial Monitor and watch try the keyboard as you wish.

Note:

There will be a different response from some keys on the keyboard.

This is caused by difference of Arduino response to the keyboard than the standard PC.

Simple Drive a 220V Relay With Arduino

This is a simple circuit for driving 220V/16A Relay with Arduino UNO.

Why use relay with Arduino?

You need to use a relay to control devices and appliances with Arduino. As you already know, Arduino- **like all Microcontrollers -** has many GPIOs have 5V output. And you need to drive devices using 220V for operation. Here comes the rule of relay. It's an electromechanical device that can be electrically controlled to control high voltage and currents.

Supplies:
12V - 220V/16A Relay

Diode

10K Ohm Resistor

2N2222 NPN Transistor

Arduino UNO

Wires

Soldering Iron

Soldering Wire

Breadboard

1mm Copper Wire

Drive a Relay With a Transistor - Transistor As a Switch

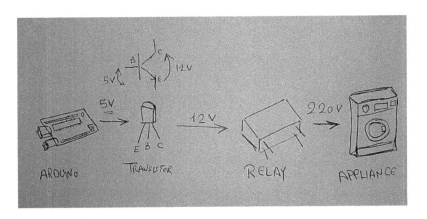

But if you want to drive a relay with Arduino here comes another challenge. Arduino GPIO output voltage is only 5V and limited current. But the relay in hand needs 12V to energize its relay and it draws large current than that what Arduino can support.

You then use transistor as a switch.

This is a powerful circuit that makes you drive a relay using Arduino with a transistor as a switch for the larger voltage and current that the relay's coil uses.

In short, you can use a 5V Output PIN from Arduino to drive a large device that is 220V operated by bootstrapping a 12V relay using a 5V operated transistor.

Circuit

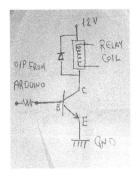

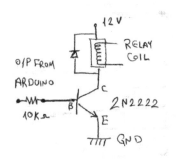

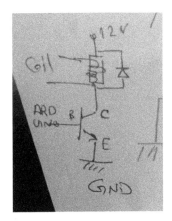

If you are like me, then you may want to take a fast look at the schematics of the circuit. So here it is.

Just a simple circuit that contains our transistor, diode, resistor and of course, the relay.

Transistor acts as a switch to control the 12V to relay coil.

Diode acts as a protection for transistor against back EMF induced through relay coil during transit conditions.

Resistor adjusts input current from Arduino to the transistor.

Get the Parts

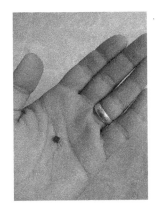

I had an old Microwave over that had its Megatron defected *(that's the most expensive part of the Microwave Oven).*

So I used parts from it in many projects. And here I used its control panel.

The relay that drives the Megatron *(Microwave Generator)* has a 12V control voltage and it can drive a 220V/16A device through its coil.

I also found a transistor that I took and used for the same purpose.

As for the diode, I found a small surface mount diode soldered under the relay on the Microwave control panel circuit board. You can see it in the photo and you can also note the diode sign on the printed board.

Prepare and Start Assembling

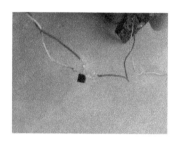

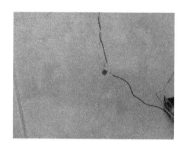

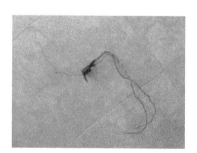

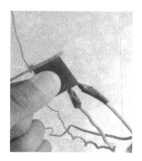

So I used the board as it is.

I used a saw to cut the printed board to get the relay and the diode with their footprints on the printed board.

And it worked great.

So I only needed to solder wires on the relay control pins. And then I connected a 1mm copper wire to the coil contacts. Those are the wires that hold the high voltage/ high current.

Connect to Arduino, Upload Software and Run the Test

Here I connected Arduino UNO Board to the circuit. I connected the 10K Ohm to the PIN 12 of Arduino UNO to get its output.

Note:

Connect relay and transistor VCC and GND to the 12V power supply and not from 5V from Arduino.

I opened Arduino IDE and then opened the famous **Blink** Example. I added 3 lines of code to add output on PIN 12 besides LED PIN 13. This makes synchronized visual and audible feedback from both LED and Relay.

Compile the sketch and upload it to Arduino.

Note that you need to modify the blink sketch to control any device without the continuous ON and OFF.

To make the relay energized:

digitalWrite(Relay, HIGH);

To make the relay de-energized:

digitalWrite(Relay, LOW);

Run and Have fun.

Clone Arduino UNO Into ATtiny85 Microcontroller

I know, this is an old and repeated project but it's still fresh and useful. Who doesn't use Arduino?

And who doesn't want to make his Arduino project permanent?

But the problem is that when you make your Arduino project permanent you are giving away your favorite Arduino board to that project and you are wasting a valuable prototyping tool for this single project.

You may go and buy another Arduino board. That's fine. But what if you could use a less expensive Microcontroller chip and a smaller footprint one?

That's exactly what happened with me when I decided to make my Arduino project permanent and on a remote area. That means that I couldn't use my Arduino UNO board anymore.

So I've decided to go through it and build my own Arduino UNO clone using this little Atmel ATtiny85 Microcontroller chip.

Install ATiny on Arduino IDE

I first made this step in a separate video to try my hand into it to get myself into action.

Note:

I'm using Arduino UNO 1.8 so it's much easier than older versions.

Just follow the following steps:

- Get the link from here and copy it.

https://raw.githubusercontent.com/damellis/attiny/ide-1.6.x-boards-manager/package_damellis_attiny_index.json

- Open **File** --> **Preferences**. Paste the link in **Additional Board Manager** text box.

- Open **Tools** --> **Board** --> **Boards Manager**

- Choose attiny and press Install

Now you have Attiny in Arduino IDE.

Programming Circuit - Connect ATtiny to Arduino UNO

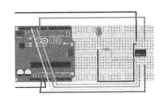

come from your PC when the Arduino software starts to program your part. Because you want to program a part further downstream, you filter the reset pulses coming into the Arduino. Otherwise, you'd invoke the Arduino's bootloader and program that Arduino, and that's not what you want at all;);

Arduino Uno – ATtiny85

5V – Vcc

Gnd – Gnd

Pin 13 – Pin 2

Pin 12 – Pin 1

Pin 11 – Pin 0

Pin 10 – Reset

And don't forget that 10uF capacitor.

GND of Arduino to Cathode

Reset of Arduino to Anode

I've read that warning that if you didn't connect the capacitor you may overwrite your Arduino UNO Bootloader by mistake.

Prepare Arduino UNO to Be an ISP Programmer

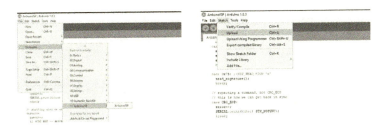

Here, you need to upload the ArduinoISP sketch on Arduino UNO board to act as an ISP Programmer.

Choose

File ---> Examples ---> 11.ArduinoISP --->
ArduinoISP

And then choose

Sketch ---> Upload

Burn the Bootloader

Now choose ATtiny 85 as follows:

Tools ---> Boards: ATtiny25/45/85

Tools ---> Processor: ATtiny85

Tools ---> Clock: Internal 8MHz

Tools ---> Programmer: Arduino as ISP

Now you are ready to burn the Arduino Bootloader on ATtiny85 as follows:

Tools ---> Burn Bootloader

First I got this error message. Then I checked the connection and it just worked fine without any error.

Upload the Blink Sketch - or Just Any Other Sketch

Now you can program ATtiny85 just as any other Arduino Board.

Just choose the desired sketch and then choose **upload**.

Note:

You need to handle the differences between Arduino UNO board and ATtiny85 Pin Mapping.

For example, In the Blink sketch, you can see that LED 13 is named LED_BuiltIn. This gives error when compiling the Blink sketch for ATtiny85 Microcontroller. So you need to change it to another PIN on ATtiny85.

Test Your New ATtiny Arduino

Now you officially have your new Arduino intelligence on a small ATtiny85 Microcontroller that costs about $2.

Now you can connect it to VCC and GND and connect the LED to PIN 0 and GND.

Connect the power to ATtiny85 Microcontroller and see it working.

Congratulations.

Connect Arduino with GSM Shield SIM900

I got this GSM Arduino shield and decided to use it and share the experiment and knowledge with you.

This is a complete beginner guide to this GSM Shield. Soon I'll be sharing some useful projects I make with this module. But in this project I'm only sharing my experiments for getting started with this module.

Supplies:

Arduino UNO

SIM900 GSM Module

Choosing Power Supply Source

The module can be powered by one of two ways:

- Separate power source.
- Power from Arduino.

You can choose the power source from the DIP switch beside the Antenna.

Typically, the module has its own power socket. So you can power it from a separate power supply of about 12V/1A or 5V/2A.

This may be the maximum power rating or the maximum input power to support the module at its maximum power demand periods - at making calls.

But you can also power the module directly from Arduino only by connecting the shield on top of Arduino like any other shield. This will make Vcc and GND of the module connected to Vcc and GND of Arduino board.

At the beginning of my experiments, I made this connection without any problems. Yes you can power this high demanding module directly from an Arduino board but this is not recommended because this module requires high power at transmission mode.

While I have been trying to try all types of code with this module I had no problem with power from Arduino.

But after a while I found that when I move the module and Arduino in different place I noticed that the power LED on the module started to faint and eventually it powers down.

At the beginning I thought there was something wrong with the module. And I even tried another SIM card from another service provider.

And then I remembered the power demand of this module so I went to another place with an open setup just as you go with your mobile phone to get a better signal for clearer voice.

So at the end of my trials with software, I decided to make my project as reliable as possible by giving the module its highest power demand from a dedicated power source.

I used a 12V/1A power adapter to power the module.

Note:

When you power the module from an external power source Arduino cannot be powered from the module. So you also need a separate power source for Arduino.

Power ON the Module and Automatic Powering

You can *Power On* and *Power OFF* the
module by pressing the Power push button for
one second.

You can do this easily every time you need to
use you module.

But what if you need to have your module
running in a remote area and you had Arduino
restarted. Then you need to automatically
Power ON the module using Software Power
ON feature.

You only need three things to use this feature:

1- You need to solder the JP Jumper on the module. This jumper enable the feature from the module hardware.

2- You need to connect Arduino PIN 9 to PIN 9 on the module and this PIN will be dedicated to that purpose exclusively.

3- You need to run the code snippet that power on the module. This code typically simulates pressing the Power push button for one second.

digitalWrite(9,HIGH);

delay(1000);

digitalWrite(9,LOW);

delay(5000);

AT Commands

You can communicate and control SIM900 GSM Module using AT commands using either *Serial()* or *SoftSerial()* functions.

There are so many useful AT commands that you can commonly use.

For Example:

- Answer incoming call
GPRS.println("ATA;");

- Hang up a call: **GPRS.println("ATH;");**

I uploaded the AT command guide here.

Receiving a Call

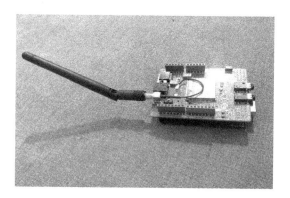

void ListenToCall()

{

// Display any text that the GSM **shield** sends
out on the serial monitor

if(GPRS.available() >0) {

// Get the character from the cellular serial port

// With an incoming call, a "RING" message is
sent out

```
incoming_char=GPRS.read();

// Check if the shield is sending a "RING"
message

if (incoming_char=='R') {

delay(10);

Serial.print(incoming_char);

incoming_char=GPRS.read();

if (incoming_char =='I') {

delay(10);

Serial.print(incoming_char);

incoming_char=GPRS.read();

if (incoming_char=='N') {
```

```
delay(10);

Serial.print(incoming_char);

incoming_char=GPRS.read();

if (incoming_char=='G') {

delay(10);

Serial.print(incoming_char);

// If the message received from the shield is
RING

Called = Called + 1 ;

delay (1000);

}

}
```

}

}

}

}

Making a Call

```
void Call_PhoneNumber()

{ GPRS.println("ATD + xxxxxxxxx;");

delay(1000);

}
```

Supply Power to Arduino

 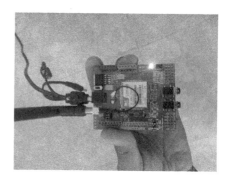

In this step we'll discuss a useful feature in this GSM Module. While you can supply it from

Arduino, it's recommended to supply it from an external source of power.

Then as we've seen that's a more reliable approach.

So you can supply the GSM Module from a 12 V power supply but you still need to supply your Arduino Board or your main Microcontroller.

In this case you may need an extra 5V power supply. Here comes that useful feature from SIM900 Module in which it can supply Arduino or Microcontroller with 4.1V and even when it is still in the OFF state.

That means it can still supply Arduino or Microcontroller as long as it's connected to its power source.

I've connected a couple of wires to the two pins indicating 4.1V and GND as shown in the image.

You can find 4.1V regulated and supplied from the shield in both OFF and ON states.

After you supply Arduino or Microcontroller from your GSM Module, Arduino or Microcontroller can power ON the Module as described in Step 3. Then you can start using the Module normally.

Conclusion

Now I hope that you have tested those simple Arduino projects and built them with your hands to get the feeling of how the whole process looks like.

I would like to hear from you on my email: *ahmed@aeroarduino.com*

And please leave an honest review for this book so I can be able to make it better.

Thank you for taking this journey with us.

www.ingramcontent.com/pod-product-compliance
Lightning Source LLC
Chambersburg PA
CBHW031244050326
40690CB00007B/945